Jack's Library

by Tirrell Anthony

Illustrated by Lane Gregory

PEARSON
Scott Foresman

Editorial Offices: Glenview, Illinois • Parsippany, New Jersey • New York, New York
Sales Offices: Needham, Massachusetts • Duluth, Georgia • Glenview, Illinois
Coppell, Texas • Sacramento, California • Mesa, Arizona

Jack loved to read a book each night.
His books were scattered, all in sight.
He read all day.
He read at night.
Sometimes he read with his flashlight.

Jack's books were here.
His books were there.
He could not even find his chair.
He could not see which clothes to wear.
"That's enough!" his mother said.
"Clean up these books and get to bed!"

"Clean them up?
But how? Right now?
I have no clue. What should I do?
Should I arrange them all by size?
Or should I just alphabetize?"

---

clue: idea or hint

arrange: put in order

"Oh, I don't know.
I'm just not clear.
How do I move them all from here?
Should I pile them on the floor?
Stack them up behind the door?
I can't think straight anymore!"

---

pile: to put one on top of the other

"Wait! What is this book I see here?
Hmmmmm . . . *How To Make A Library!*
I can organize by author's name—
That sounds like a real cool game!
Arrange them like the alphabet.
That sounds easy. That's no sweat!
Or I could organize by title too.
I realize now that's what I will do!"

---

no sweat: easy

"All *A* titles I'll put here.
Followed by the *B's* right there.
This is great! Now I see!
Next will come the spot for *C.*
This is really so much fun!"
Following these rules of thumb,
Jack organized them one by one.
He sorted them all from *A* to *Z.*
He organized them happily.

---

rules of thumb: simple ways

His mother was surprised and impressed.
She never thought he'd pass that test.
But Jack came through after all
And shelved his books up on the wall.
"Books are great," said Jack with glee.
"They helped me make a library!"

came through: succeeded

glee: happiness

The nine stories in the debut collection, *Wolf Note*, thrust the reader into diverse worlds from San Francisco in the 1940s to the tangled imagination of a delusional adolescent in a contemporary mental ward, introducing characters with compassion, humor, and nuanced psychological insight. The stories capture moments in women's lives as they lose themselves—and find themselves—in love, friendship, music, and madness.

Several stories in the collection show art as a refuge and solace. An injured ballerina turns to her grandmother's Kodak camera and its 35 millimeter film, which sounds to her "like artillery ammunition," when she can no longer dance. In the title story, the narrator ponders the concept that "certain weaknesses run in families," and she embraces the cello as her brother had clung his violin. "After a few weeks, sleeping in my brother's too cold bed, I began to hear messages whispered in the cello's voice. I walked barefoot through the dark house to the music room and stood in the doorway, my thighs pressed tightly together. For another moment I would deny them the delicious intimacy of the curved wood. On a small oriental carpet sat a straight-backed chair and an empty music stand. A duet of moonlight and streetlight poured through the open drapes and outlined the body of the cello lying on its side. It waited for me with the swelled hips and graceful waist of an odalisque beckoning from a divan."

These are riveting stories, full of mystery and shadows and strange, intriguing passions. Jacobs' lush, musical prose illuminates the dark corners, revealing new, at times startling, truths about family, friendship and love. A mesmerizing, assured collection.
—Cynthia Weiner, author of the 2006 Pushcart-Prize-winning story "Boyfriends."

Wolf Note is a little jewel, peopled with fascinating characters and deeply wrought emotions. Libby Jacobs' stories will stay with you long after you have turned the last page. These stories are at times mystical, sensual, and disturbing, and always beautifully written. Good writing is such a joy, and *Wolf Note* is damned good writing. Short story writing is a difficult and demanding craft, and Libby Jacobs clearly has mastered it. Light a fire, curl up, and get set to immerse yourself in the moods and power of *Wolf Note*.
—Michael Palmer, author of eleven *New York Times* Bestsellers, including *The Society, Fatal,* and *The Patient*.

From the first page you know you are in the hands of a masterful, wonderful and evocative author who delves deeply into her characters and has command of nuance and style. The stories in the collection are mysterious and moving and memorable. I was enchanted.
—M. J. Rose, internationally bestselling author of six novels, including *The Halo Effect, The Delilah Complex,* and *The Venus Fix*.

ISBN-13: 978-0-9792091-0-9
ISBN-10: 0-9792091-0-2
51495
9 780979 209109

Rager Media
Akron, Ohio
www.ragermedia.com
RagerMedia,Inc.